D0926554

# TECHNOLOGY IN ACTION

# SPORTS TECHNOLOGY

**Neil Duncanson**

MAC KILLOP SCHOOL LIBRARY

## Titles in this series

Aircraft Technology

Building Technology

Camera Technology

Car Technology

Energy Technology

Farming Technology

Food Technology

Information Technology

Medical Technology

Military Technology

Ship Technology

Spacecraft Technology

Sports Technology

Train Technology

TV and Video Technology

Undersea Technology

First published in 1991 by
Wayland (Publishers) Ltd
61 Western Road, Hove
East Sussex BN3 1JD, England

© Copyright 1991 Wayland (Publishers) Ltd

Series Editor: William Wharfe
Book Editor: Paul Bennett
Designer: David Armitage

**British Library Cataloguing in Publication Data**
Duncanson, Neil
    Sports technology. – (Technology in action)
    I. Title. II. Series
    796.028

ISBN 0-7502-0131-2

Typeset by Direct Image Photosetting Limited,
Sussex, England
Printed in Italy by G. Canale & C.S.p.A., Turin
Bound in France by A.G.M.

**Cover**  Skiers have benefited from plastic and synthetic materials, which have made skis lighter and easier to manoeuvre.

# Contents

**Above** Technological advances in motorsports have increased speeds *and* safety.
Some of today's powerboats are capable of speeds in excess of 220 kph.

The popularity of sport has never been greater than it is today, and the signs are that its power and influence will increase into the next century.

The twentieth century has seen many changes in the way sports are played and the number of people who watch them. Television has turned many sports into giant businesses able to rival any multi-national company.

Where sport was once a weekend pastime that did not warrant technological interest, today it has the financial power and marketing appeal to demand and receive all that modern technology can offer. The companies who can supply this modern technology benefit by using sports coverage as a shop window for their products.

Sportsmen and sportswomen now compete for massive prizes and demand the best of everything, from training programmes, equipment and sportswear, to timing equipment and the best surfaces on which to perform. For their part, the paying public, with a wide variety of leisure interests from which to choose, also want the best. They want the best stadia and the best television coverage so that they can watch their favourite sports played at the highest level.

The application of practical and mechanical sciences to sports has intensified as the twentieth century has progressed and will continue to improve sporting standards for those who enjoy taking part in sports and those who enjoy watching.

A floodlit international cricket match at Australia's Sydney Cricket Ground.
Spectators want the best stadia so that they can watch their favourite sports
played at the highest level.

Sports arenas were built by many early civilizations. For example, the Romans built the first indoor stadium, the Colosseum, in Rome, between about AD70 and AD82. The remains of the giant oval structure, where ancient games and gladiatorial combat took place, can still be seen today. The Romans were well ahead of their time. In Britain, it was not until the nineteenth century that purpose-built indoor facilities began to appear. London's Royal Albert Hall, which was opened in 1871, was built to hold events such as concerts and sports tournaments, and the domed building is still used today for all kinds of sports, including boxing and basketball.

The site of Madison Square Garden, in New York, USA, one of the world's best-known arenas, was originally an outdoor venue for Barnum's Circus. It was covered in 1879 and could hold 11,000 spectators, but it was demolished ten years later to be replaced by a $3 million auditorium. However, in 1925 a new Madison Square Garden opened nearby, which was able to hold more than 18,000 people. It quickly became a popular venue for sports events and in 1946 more than five million people attended sports events there.

**Left** Wembley Stadium – the focus of a huge sports and leisure complex.

The present Madison Square Garden opened in 1968, with a 20,000 seat arena, 48 lane bowling alley, exhibition hall, 5,000 seat forum, and 11 escalators, together with its own police force and TV station. The evolution of 'The Garden' is a good example of how sports arenas have developed down the years to accommodate an increasing number of events and a larger number of spectators.

Wembley Stadium, the home of British soccer, was opened in 1923 and had become something of a sporting dinosaur, for stadia should offer more than just the chance for

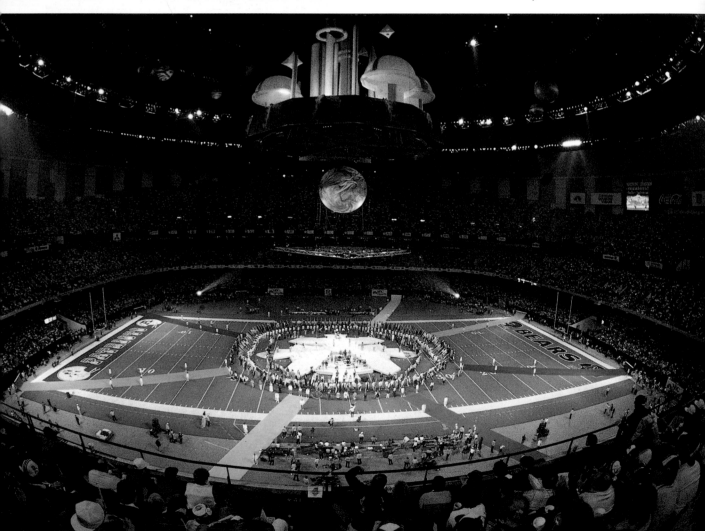

spectators to watch sports. A major overhaul that includes restaurants, special executive boxes and suites, a museum and many other attractions, is nearing completion. Further plans include a new access for the local underground railway station, improvements

**Right** Toronto's SkyDome is the world's first major stadium with a fully retractable roof. It is constructed from three steel arches with a skin of PVC plastic on a steel deck. The illustration shows how the roof retracts in just twenty minutes. SkyDome is enormous – the roof spans 205 m at its widest point and is thirty-one storeys high.

**Opposite** The multi-million dollar New Orleans Superdome, the venue of Superbowl XX – the American football final.

Ancient and modern – Rome's Colosseum (completed in AD 80) would fit inside SkyDome.

to the concourse, better facilities for mothers and the disabled, an indoor stadium for sports and music events, plus a hotel and conference centre. These developments will bring Wembley's facilities in line with the world's other great sporting venues.

The newly-built arenas are futuristic in their design. When the Houston Astrodome opened in Houston, USA, in 1965, it was described as the 'ninth wonder of the world'. Its steel dome and $24 million price tag made it the focus of much media attention, and it became home to the Houston Oilers football team, the Astros baseball team and many other sports. But even this famous stadium has been bettered, first by the New Orleans Superdome in the USA, which opened in 1976, costing $121 million and seating 80,000 people under its own steel dome; and then by Canada's Toronto SkyDome.

The computer-designed, thirty-one storey high SkyDome was opened in 1989, at a cost of more than $500 million, and was immediately heralded as the most innovative stadium ever built. Its huge roof can be opened or closed in just twenty minutes, and so events can take place regardless of the weather. Its leisure facilities are of the highest standards and it is billed as 'the world's greatest entertainment centre'.

The SkyDome is expected to revolutionize the design of stadia, and its attractions include a 350-room hotel with 70 suites overlooking the pitch. It boasts restaurants, bars, health and fitness facilities, such as a pool and squash courts, a TV studio, the world's biggest video scoreboard (35 m × 10 m) and 161 private boxes. The seating is movable and is so arranged that up to 65,000 spectators can have an unobstructed view of sports events.

The SkyDome has set the standard for stadium design and it is no coincidence that when it was opened, the publicity included a note that Rome's ancient Colosseum could fit neatly inside it!

# Equipment

**3**

In the competitive environment of today's professional sports millions of pounds are spent trying to help players find 'the edge' – that small improvement that means the difference between winning or losing. The technological development of sports equipment is helping them to reach for even higher goals.

Up to the 1980s, the world's great tennis players had used wooden rackets. But wooden rackets were not strong enough for the new generation of powerful hitters, such as Jimmy Connors, Ivan Lendl and Boris Becker – something new had to be found.

Old-style rackets could not have coped with Boris Becker's power.

At first, attempts were made to strengthen wood, often with plastic, but this made the rackets too heavy. Scientists then came up with what became known as graphite rackets, which are made from carbon fibre. These are specially reinforced with a material called Kevlar, which is more commonly used in the manufacture of bullet-proof vests and ceramic fibres. Today's rackets weigh around 320 g, with the heaviest component being the glue that holds all the parts together!

British technology has also come up with an injection-moulded racket where nylon and graphite granules are injected into a mould

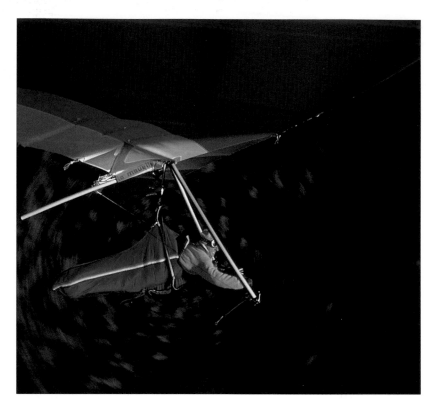

Using a body bag, a hang-glider pilot can fly for hours without getting cold.

**Below** The parts of a hang-glider. Hang-gliders come in various shapes and sizes – some even look like conventional aircraft.

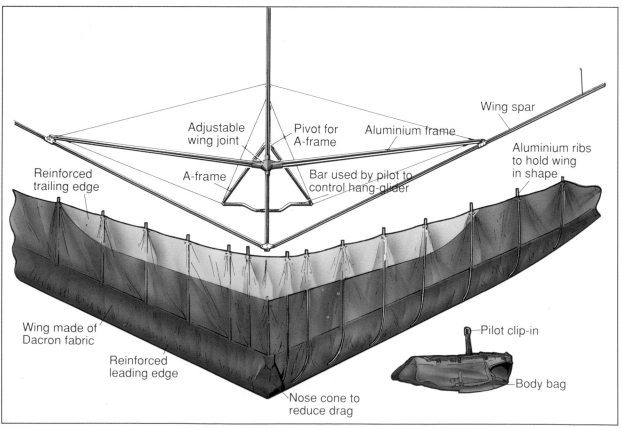

Adjustable wing joint

Pivot for A-frame

Aluminium frame

Wing spar

Aluminium ribs to hold wing in shape

Reinforced trailing edge

A-frame

Bar used by pilot to control hang-glider

Wing made of Dacron fabric

Reinforced leading edge

Pilot clip-in

Body bag

Nose cone to reduce drag

In the physically demanding sport of American football, the players need the best protection.

which then sets like a cake. The key is lightness and strength, and so far technology has been able to find the solutions to the problems posed by men's tennis.

A similar problem was encountered in professional golf, with the advent of more skilled players and harder hitters. Old style golf clubs were made from one piece of wood, usually hickory, and since the 1930s steel-shafted clubs have been popular. Graphite clubs are a recent development. Mostly cast from standard moulds, the shafts are specially made and balanced for individual clubs. Even the 'woods' are now made of plastic-coated metal.

Golf balls have also developed greatly. The original 'feathery' ball was a leather bag crammed with goose feathers that had been soaked in water, which was sewn up and when it dried it became rock hard. In 1899, Dr Coburn Haskell from Cleveland, Ohio, USA, invented a ball which had a hard rubber shell packed with elastic. The Haskell ball survived into the 1960s. But the players began to ask for a ball that gave them more control, particularly for spin. Several have been developed and the newest is the Bolata ball consisting of a rubber coating around a centre of water or paste. The ball allows players to play shots with more dexterity, although to the amateur it is more difficult to hit a long way.

Some major developments have come in the physically demanding sport of American football, where the players need eighteen pieces of protective gear. Until the 1940s, footballers wore flimsy leather helmets. They afforded very little protection and, as a result, there were a number of deaths. An American firm, the John T Riddell Company, which manufactured pilot's helmets, then developed a plastic football helmet which was adopted by the American Football League in the 1940s – all players were required to wear these helmets. Within ten years the 'teardrop'

helmet evolved – the type of helmet that is still used today. The face guard, or 'cage', came into general use in the 1950s. Most of today's players wear helmets with air-filled pockets, which are inflated when a player has the helmet on his head to ensure that it fits snugly and to provide cushioning.

As the game became more competitive in the 1960s, due in part to television coverage of games and increasing sponsorship, the players began to ask for all kinds of extra protection. Mouthguards, nylon shoulder pads, rib, arm and leg protectors and neck rolls, plus metres of protective tape around joints came into use. In 1978, the inflatable rib protector was invented.

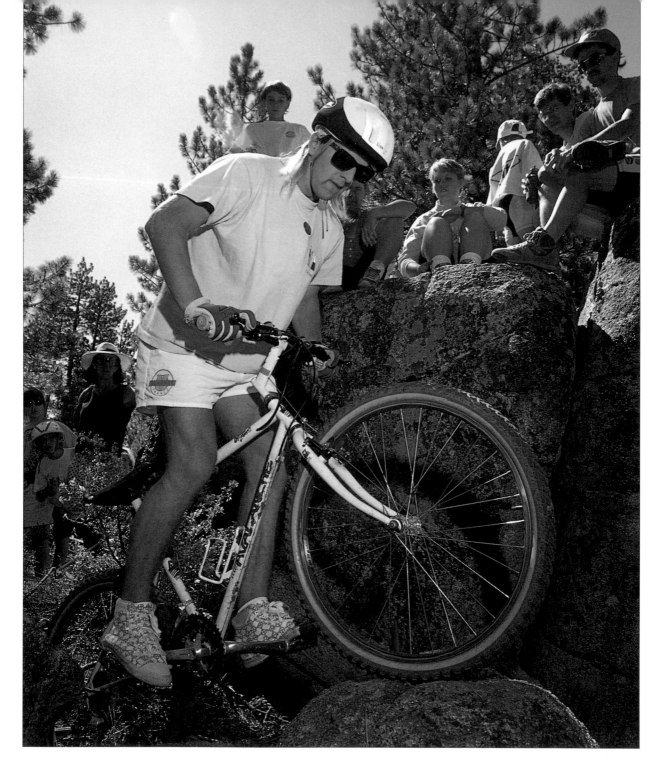

Mountain biking is one of the fastest-growing sports. It combines the speed of cycling on the road with the freedom to travel across the roughest country.

Bicycling has always been a popular sport. In the mid-1970s, BMX bikes were the rage. BMX stands for bicycle motocross, and the bicycles were built for stunt riding over an obstacle course. Mountain bikes then started to become popular in the early 1980s, and today,

Skin-tight Lycra suit

Aero helmet

Tinted visor

Heart-beat monitor and transmitter

Handlebar computer

Aero bars

Tri-spoke wheel

Gear levers

Ultra-thin tyres

Rear block of 8 sprockets

Shoe plate

Plastic shoes

Two front chain rings

The parts of a modern aerodynamic racing bicycle. The frames of some bicycles are made of a lightweight material called carbon fibre.

about 45 per cent of all bikes sold are mountain bikes.

Mountain bikes are designed to travel over very difficult terrain. The pioneers, Gary Fisher and Charlie Kelly, from Marin County, California, made their bikes from whatever parts they could find on the garage floor. Heavy-duty parts are the feature of these bikes. Large, wide tyres absorb the shock of rough ground, heavy wheel rims give strength and prevent wheel-buckling, 18-speed derailleur gears are essential for travelling up and down steep slopes, and the strong frame has to have the necessary clearances for the wide tyres.

Mountain bikes are very different compared with the lightweight bicycles used by track and time-trial cyclists. In one design, the bicycle frame is made of carbon fibre and the tri-spoke wheels of moulded Kevlar – disc wheels are sometimes used, but these are a disadvantage in windy conditions. 'Aero bars' give the rider an aerodynamic position on the bicycle.

The rider will wear a Lycra suit and a streamlined helmet, and will shave his or her legs to reduce wind resistance. The shoes are made of plastic with rigid carbon soles and built-in shoeplates. These plates have slots which fit into the backplate of the pedal and fasten in place with clamps very similar to ski-boot bindings. A handlebar computer gives the distance the cyclist has travelled and the rider's speed. A heart-beat monitor will record the cyclist's pulse rate, which will later be analysed for training purposes.

Comfort and ease of movement are essential elements of any type of sports clothing. The tracksuit in athletics became popular in the early 1920s, and little changed in terms of athletes' vests and shorts until the 1980s, when figure-hugging bodysuits, made from a synthetic, elastic fabric called Lycra, appeared. The Lycra suits cut wind resistance, and help to keep leg muscles and tendons warm, thus reducing the risk of injury while the athlete is performing. Lycra bodysuits are now used by many different sportsmen and sportswomen. Racing cyclists, swimmers and downhill skiers use the suits to help improve their performances.

Protection from the elements is also important. Golfers and mountaineers, for example, need to keep dry and comfortable when it is windy or raining. Up to the late 1970s, water and windproof fabrics were either cotton or nylon that had been coated with an impervious layer of either wax or rubber.

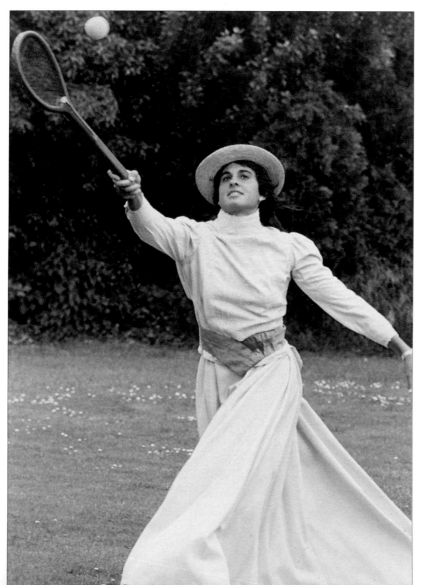

Modern day Argentinian tennis star, Gabriela Sabatini, in nineteenth-century tennis clothes. Sports clothing design has come a long way in the last 100 years.

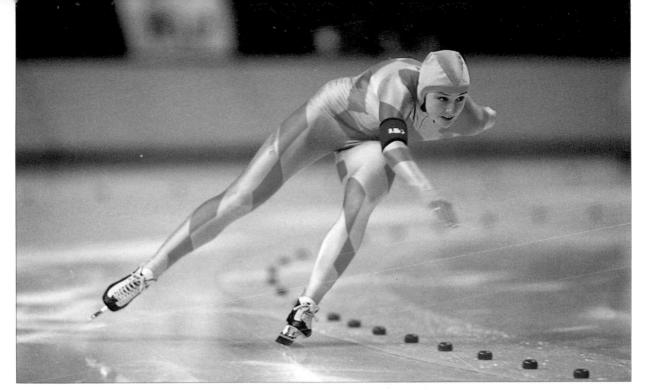

**Above** Speed skaters are among the many sports stars who rely on Lycra to cut wind resistance.

**Right** GORE-TEX, a fabric that 'breathes', was invented in 1977.

The problem with these fabrics was that they did not allow perspiration from the body to escape, and so the sportsman or sportswoman might end up as 'wet' inside the clothing as it was outside.

In 1977, a 'breathable' fabric was invented by an American, Bob Gore. Called GORE-TEX Fabric, it normally consists of three layers: between the outer fabric and the lining is a membrane of PTFE – a material that has been engineered to contain 9 billion pores per 2.5 sq cm. Each pore is 20,000 times smaller than a droplet of water, which forms an impenetrable barrier to wind, rain and snow.

Yet each pore is 700 times larger than a vapour molecule, allowing pespiration to escape from the body.

Breathable and waterproof fabrics are made into jackets, trousers, gloves, hats, socks, backpacks, tents and sleeping bags for a variety of sports activities, including athletics, skiing, golf, climbing, canoeing and cycling.

The wetsuit is worn by men and women who practise their sport on or under water. Made from neoprene – a rubber-based material – they come in many shapes and sizes, including a one-piece suit with short arms and legs (a 'shorty'), a suit with long arms and legs (a 'full' wetsuit) and a combination of the two.

Wetsuits are worn to keep the body warm – when people get so cold that their body temperature drops below normal, a very serious condition known as hypothermia results, which can be fatal if prolonged. Neoprene itself is waterproof, but most kinds of stitching are not. The more waterproof a wetsuit is, the warmer the person will be. In some wetsuits the panels are glued and 'blind-stitched' – the neoprene is stitched through on one side only and has a 'bead' of rubber sealant to glue the seams together. The thickness of the suit is important, too – 5 mm-thick neoprene is warmer than 3 mm-thick neoprene. Often wetsuits are lined with Lycra to give a colourful and hard-wearing outer skin.

However, perhaps the greatest leap forward in sportswear technology has been in footwear. In the early days, there were no training shoes, just boots for specific sports, such as soccer, cricket, athletics and so on.

The uppers were all made of leather, with weighty leather or rubber soles and were all very heavy and cumbersome.

One of the leading shoe companies in the world is Adidas, which, under the guidance of founder Adi Dassler, began making sports shoes in the 1920s. Dassler's main tasks were to reduce their weight and improve both protection for the foot against injury, and durability.

By 1937 Dassler's range of shoes included thirty different models, and after the Second World War he founded the Adidas company and pioneered the soccer boot with a moulded sole for icy grounds, and then the revolutionary screw-in studs. Adi Dassler then went on to develop replaceable spikes and shock absorption in track shoes, both of which were used in the 1952 Olympics.

Throughout the 1950s and 1960s, new, lightweight materials, such as nylon, were used in the manufacture of sports shoes and today more than fifty stages are used in the design process of a new shoe. These stages include key areas such as research, design, making a sample, durability testing, costing and bulk production, followed by delivery across the world.

Sports shoes are big business and a major part of the budgets of shoe manufacturers is spent encouraging top sportsmen and sportswomen to wear their products, particularly at major sporting events such as the World Cup and the Olympics. From the steel toe-capped, water-sodden, heavy boots of the past, technology has created the super-lightweight, highly protective, adaptable and fashionable shoes of today.

**Opposite** Breathable fabrics form an impenetrable barrier to rain and snow, yet allow perspiration to escape from the body, preventing clamminess. For many outdoor sports, clothing made from breathable fabric is now seen as essential.

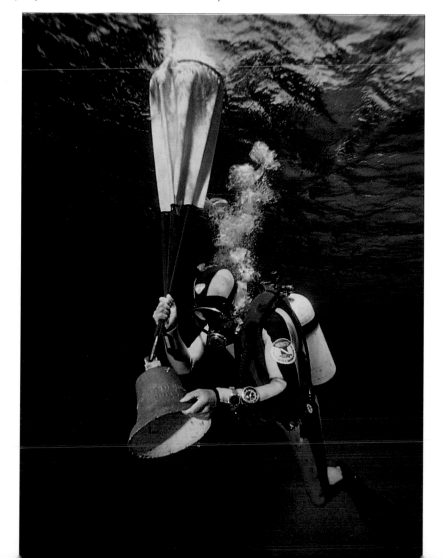

**Right** Wetsuits are designed to protect divers from the cold.

The development of the wetsuit in the 1950s and 1960s enabled the spread of the exciting sport of surfing from warm seas to cold seas. The Polynesian islanders of the central Pacific were probably the first to ride waves – the famous explorer, Captin Cook, wrote about

Batten pockets with battens

Mylar sail

Mast

PVC/monofilm window

Boom

Wetsuit

Mast track    Mast foot

Seat harness

Board made of lightweight foam core covered with glassfibre

Retractable daggerboard

Footstraps

Fin

**Above** The top women's surfer, Wendy Botha, during a surfing contest.
Surfboards are made from lightweight plastic materials which make them
manoeuvrable.

**Opposite** A windsurfing board. Shortboards do not have daggerboards.
They are highly manoeuvrable and can be used for jumping off waves (inset).

the skill of the Hawaiians in 1778. In those days, surfboards were made of solid wood, which were extremely heavy and difficult to manoeuvre. The innovations in plastics since the Second World War have revolutionized the sport. Plastic materials are also used in the making of windsurfing boards, the idea of which was first dreamt up in the late 1950s.

Surfboards and windsurfing boards have a light-weight foam core covered with glassfibre or a similar material. Windsurfing boards often have reinforcement from materials such as carbon fibre or Kevlar, to produce boards which are light, stiff and reasonably durable.

There are two basic types of windsurfing boards: longboards with a daggerboard (a big, removable fin in the middle which stops the board going sideways when sailing upwind), and shortboards which are too short to build daggerboards into their hulls. Longboards are ideal for beginners. Special longboards are used for racing. Shortboards are very manoeuvrable and require a higher level of expertise to ride them.

Skiing is a perpetual quest for speed – every year ski manufacturers seem to come up with a new technological innovation which will improve the performance of ski equipment.

Most masts are made of glassfibre, although those for racing are more often made of aluminium, which is lighter and stiffer. Many sails are made of a synthetic material called Mylar, which is light, durable and waterproof. Windows in the sail help the windsurfer to see where he or she is going and to avoid hazards, such as other windsurfers. PVC/monofilm – a type of plastic – is often used for the window.

Every year, ski manufacturers seem to find new ways to make ski equipment perform just a little better. Plastic and synthetic materials have made skis lighter and easier to manoeuvre. One latest design has a fibreglass core protected with a plastic elastomer – a material that is able to bend without breaking. To help in turning and stopping, skis have steel edges which can be dug into the snow.

Slalom skis are narrower than other types of skis, as they are best for making quick turns. Some come with bent tips, which help to deflect the gate poles as the skier threads his or her way down the course.

Ski boots have changed dramatically since the 1960s, when people skied in boots that were really modified hiking boots. These boots were not altogether comfortable or easy to put on and take off. Modern ski boots are basically a plastic shell which can be put on either from the back or front. Front-entry types fasten by means of a padded tongue tightened by buckles, and are very popular with racers. Rear-entry boots are fastened with a hinged flap and use various methods of keeping the heel down inside the boot.

Good binding design has almost halved skiing injuries over the last fifteen years. The bindings are spring-loaded clamps that are attached to the skis, which hold down the ski boots. If the skier falls heavily, the binding springs open to release the boot from the ski.

Snowboarding is the newest snow sport. Instead of wearing two skis, the snowboarder uses a single, wide board that is between about 140 and 165 cm in length (skis are about 180 to 190 cm in length). Racing boards are longer and stiffer than freestyle boards

Technology is already helping the new sport of snowboarding.

designed for doing jumps and tricks. 'Soft boots' give freedom of movement and comfort and are used with freestyle boards. 'Hard boots' give support and are used with racing boards. The boots and bindings are similar to their conventional skiing counterparts, except that the bindings do not have a quick release feature.

A few weeks before the opening of the 1988 Olympics a 200 strong team of men and women, together with hundreds of tonnes of equipment, arrived in the South Korean capital of Seoul to begin their preparations for the Games. Not a surprising fact, given that almost every nation sent a team to take part in the world's greatest sporting event. But this team of people was simply there to time those who were competing and not to compete themselves. The team comprised official time-keepers, scientists, computer wizards and technical magicians from the giant Swiss company, Omega.

The planning and organization involved in timing the Olympics is a far cry from the days when officials used stopwatches and clip-boards to do their timing. Electronic timing has been used intermittently since the 1930s,
but it was not officially adopted by athletics authorities until 1977.

In Seoul, computers were used to create what was, in fact, a 'fourth dimension' in time and picture. The starting gun was wired to the starting blocks, which were fitted with sensitive pads, so that a computer could detect which athlete had made a false start. In addition, the gun triggered three cameras, two on the outside and one on the inside of the track, which took continuous exposure of the 100 m race, to produce a kind of 'time picture'. The moment the race finished judges and timekeepers had the finishing times displayed on television screens and the electronic scoreboard, but close scrutiny of the time picture enabled them to check the times for each athlete to a thousandth of a second.

All time-based sports make use of electronic

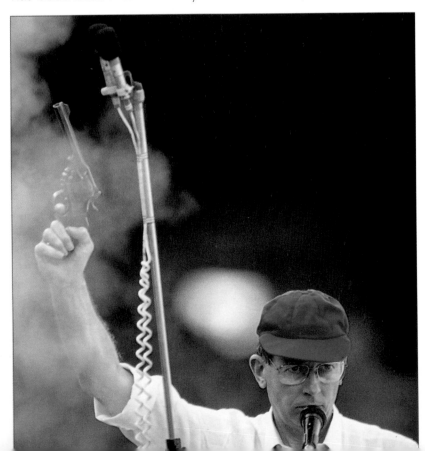

The starter's gun and sprinters' starting blocks are wired to a timing computer, which acts as a false start control system, and gives timing of incredible accuracy.

technology to achieve timing of incredible accuracy. In Formula One motor racing, the timekeepers set up mini television stations around each Grand Prix circuit. Transmitters are carried in each car and relay information to specially-located timing points on the circuit. These measure the speed of the car and assess lap times, down to a thousandth of a second, which are then relayed to television screens in the pits, to the media and crowd.

At the Calgary Winter Olympics in 1988, a system was devised to measure the bobsleigh event, and no less than eighty special sensors were set up along the course. These were linked to a computer that could calculate the speed of each bobsleigh at any stage of the course, so that afterwards the crews could

A time picture – the exact moment a race is won captured on film.

analyse on which part of the course they could improve their performance. Swimming pools are now built to accommodate pressure-sensitive timing pads, which are attached to each end of the pool. The pads are 1 cm thick and so an extra 2 cm are added to the length of the pool. The pads are wired to a computer which gives incredibly accurate times for each swimming lane.

Timing is very important when a split-second can mean the difference between winning and losing. Once again technology has responded well to the changing and growing demands of sports.

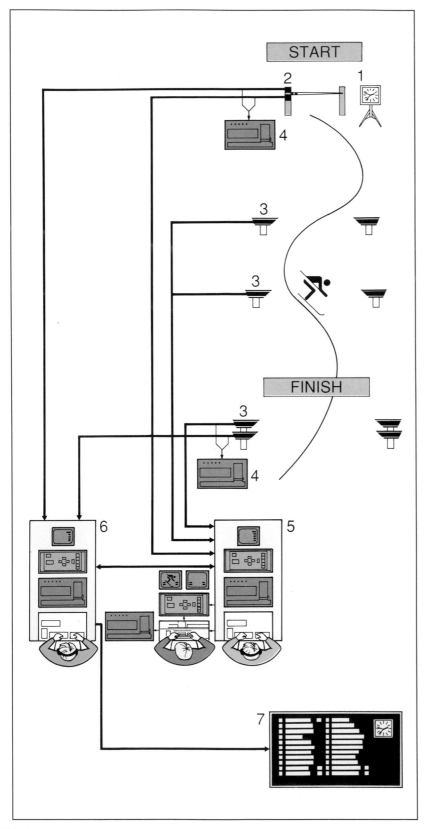

START

FINISH

Modern timing systems can calculate the actual time of a competitor to one ten-thousandth of a second and automatically give his or her ranking during an event. The illustration shows the system used at a skiing event.

1. The synchronized start clock indicates the start to the competitor both visually and with sound.
2. When the skier goes through the start gate, it gives two simultaneous electrical impulses.
3. Photoelectric cells record the skier's time at various stages of a downhill course and a final time.
4. Two synchronized electronic counters are used in case of breakdown of the lines.
5. The principal timing control unit distributes timing information to the scoreboard, TV control room and to the race officials.
6. Back-up timing control unit in case of a breakdown to the main timing control unit.
7. Scoreboard.

It has always been a challenge to find ways of improving an athlete's performance. At the Seoul Olympics, Canada's Ben Johnson 'won' the 100 m in 9.79 seconds – with a peak speed of about 43.5 kph. But when it was discovered that he had been taking performance-enhancing drugs, he was disqualified and stripped of his gold medal and record time. America's second placed Carl Lewis became the champion in a time of 9.92 seconds, with a peak speed of about 42.5 kph.

**Above** High-tech starting blocks have helped runners to take off faster.

The start of the 100 m at the 1936 Berlin Olympics. Note the cinder track.

At the first Olympics, the winning time was exactly 12 seconds, but since then much has happened to enable athletes to run faster. That first Olympic final was held on a cinder track, with the athletes either standing or crouching with their feet in shallow holes which they had dug to give them a firm start. Today, starting blocks have replaced the holes. Patented in the 1920s, the blocks did not come into widespread use until after the Second World War and were not used at the Olympics until the London Games in 1948. Modern blocks are adjustable and are made from aluminium or zinc-plated steel, with rubber-faced footplates set at an angle to reduce the stress on the athlete's legs as he or she 'springs' into the race.

Tracks have also helped athletes to improve their times, and today's springier synthetic surfaces are ideal for the sprinter. They were

**Left** The USA's Florence Griffith-Joyner's 100 m world record time of 10.49 seconds in 1988 exceeded all expectations.

**Opposite** Today's swimwear is made to help swimmers move fast through the water.

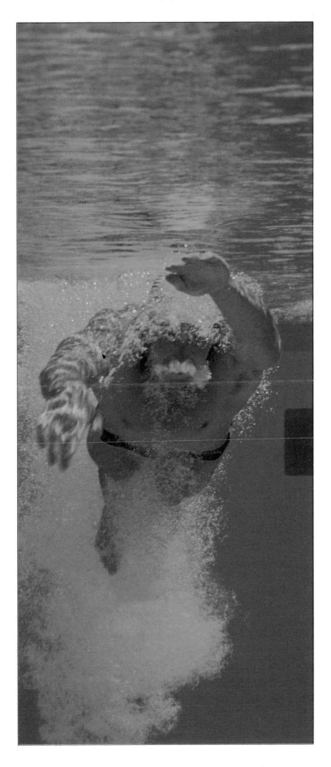

of the new, skin-tight Lycra suits, which cut down wind resistance.

In 1980, a science convention in Manchester, England, devised a complex equation in order to predict at what time in the future, and by how much, athletics records would be set. The equation took into account such things as the energy of the runner, air resistance, altitude and running tracks. At the time, the scientists predicted that the world record for the men's 100 m in the year 2000 would be 9.82 seconds (a figure already surpassed by Johnson), and for the women's 100 m a time of 10.77 seconds (already surpassed by Florence Griffith-Joyner's 10.49 seconds in 1988).

Scientists have discovered that women's times in a variety of sports have improved at a faster rate than men's times. Today, women skate as fast as men did in 1960, and swim as fast as men in 1968. One reason that has been put forward for this trend is that women have not had the benefit of competing at an international level until relatively recently. In athletics, many race distances were not added to the Olympic programme until the 1980s.

Speeds have improved in other events, such as cycling, skiing and rowing. Much of this improvement is put down to improved training and better equipment.

Swimmers' times have improved dramatically too. The men's 100 m freestyle was won in 1 minute 22.2 seconds at the first Olympics, in 1896. In Seoul, America's giant Matt Biondi won in 48.63 seconds. Studies in hydrodynamics, a branch of science concerned with the properties of liquids, have attempted to eliminate the drag of water on the body, and helped improve the efficiency of swimmers, enabling them to go faster.

Modern swimwear – made from Lycra – is designed to reduce drag. Swimmers also shave their bodies before competition to make them more streamlined, and they wear goggles to enable them to see more clearly and so anticipate turns better. Antiwave ropes, which separate the lanes, cut down wash from neighbouring swimmers in competition.

first used at the 1968 Mexico Olympics, replacing the old-style cinder tracks. In addition, athletes also have better coaching and training regimens, and have the advantage

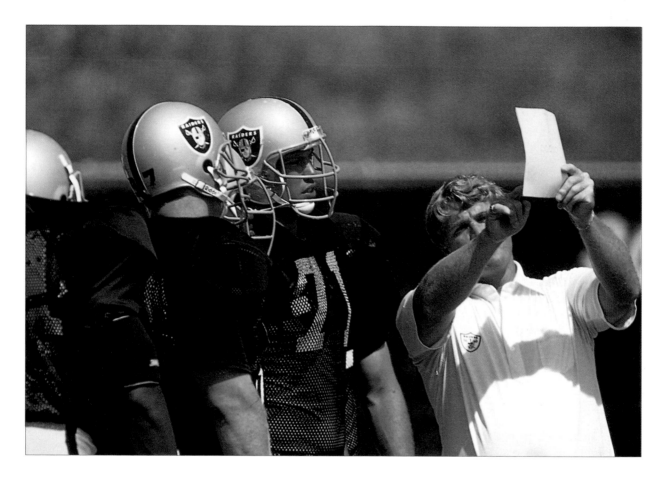

**Above** Los Angeles Raiders linemen study defensive strategy at their training headquarters.

**Opposite** English runner, Matthew Yates, undergoes some scientific race preparation.

It is no coincidence that as science has become more closely involved in sport in recent years, training techniques have improved radically. Everyone is much more health and fitness conscious these days, and many people are prepared to work much harder on their personal fitness, diet and mental approach.

At the turn of the century, this combination would have been looked upon as complete lunacy. In athletics, training was limited to running and massage, and many athletes relied on their innate ability rather than good coaching methods. There were professional coaches, but only those who were wealthy could benefit from an expert's tuition. Today, many nations can boast a vast network of coaching expertise for a wide variety of sports.

In some professional sports, there are a variety of coaches for a single team, each specializing in a particular area. For example, in the USA's National Football League, teams boast an array of coaches for the offence, defence, the quarterback, special teams and receivers. The teams also have an army of scouts to search for new talent in the high schools and colleges.

American sport has led the way in sports psychology, where mental toughness is as much a part of the sporting armour as physical training and ability. Cus D'Amato, a legendary boxing manager, always stressed that fights were won and lost in the head. He ought to know. He managed two of America's world champions, Floyd Patterson and Mike Tyson. Based on skill and physical preparation, Mike Tyson should never have lost his undisputed world title to James 'Buster' Douglas, in Tokyo,

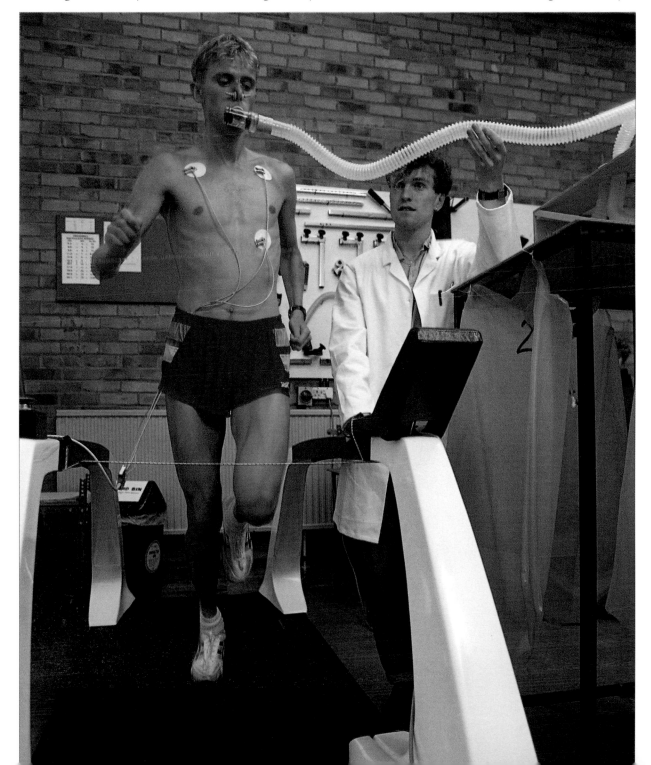

in 1990. He now admits he was not prepared mentally, and therefore his performance suffered.

Sports psychologists began by looking at the excuses sportsmen and sportswomen used for bad performances, such as loss of concentration, lack of aggression, or phrases such as 'I talked myself out of it', or 'I just wasn't feeling right today.' The key to a winning mind is to root out self-doubt and improve concentration through visualization – actually running through in your mind what you want to do and how you want to play. Jack Nicklaus, an American who is arguably the world's greatest ever golfer, never played a shot in his life without first running it through in his mind. He described it as 'going to the movies in my head'.

Many top sportsmen and sportswomen have their own psychologists to sharpen their minds before major events. Now there are no excuses and every top sporting performance is analysed both physically and mentally.

Another facet of sports preparation that has improved dramatically is nutrition – a proper sporting diet. It is not a new idea that the right food and drink aids performance, but technological advances in nutritional science and its application to the needs of different sports has meant it can make a discernible difference.

**Right** Computer technology is playing an increasing role in the training programmes of sportsmen and sportswomen. Here, a computer is used to measure performance during weight-training.

**Opposite** Jack Nicklaus is a great exponent of 'visualization' – a method of improving concentration by forming a mental image of what you want to do.

Before the 1920 Olympics 100 m sprint final, the four American sprinters each drank a glass of sherry and a raw egg – a crude stimulant aimed at giving them a bit of extra pep before the race. It obviously paid dividends because they finished first, second, fourth and sixth.

Today, sports nutritionists can design energy-giving menus for different athletes, depending on their sport and how they train for it. They insist that the right food, allied to an intake of food supplements (extra vitamins and minerals), can develop the right body for the right sport.

The nutritionists calculate the number of calories used by different athletes when they take part in their sport, and draw up a complementary menu comprising fresh foods. For example, a lunch of 100 g of cheese, a mixed salad, chips, a glass of orange juice, a banana and a cup of coffee, comes to 965 calories – enough to power a sprinter flat out for eighteen minutes or an archer for more than thirteen hours. Nutritionists look for a menu of around 3,000 to 4,000 calories each day, plus the vitamins, minerals and supplements the athlete needs.

31

In terms of pure technology, few sports have moved forward as fast as motorsport. Motorsport has been used as the testing ground for new designs of engines, bodies and chassis of racing cars, motorbikes and speed boats – if proved successful, the innovations are incorporated in production models.

The first official motor competition took place in 1894, on a dusty road between Paris and Rouen in France, where the winner completed the 127 km course with an average speed of 18.6 kph. Interest in racing then rocketed and Britain's first purpose-built race track, called Brooklands, was built in 1906. The first Grand Prix was staged at Le Mans in France in the same year and organizers had to impose a weight limit of 992 kg because the cars were getting so big. The engine sizes also grew larger and during the 1920s limits were imposed on their size.

The angular shape of the family car causes turbulance over the rear of the car.

The racing car's aerodynamic shape allows air to flow over it without causing turbulance.

**Left** The performance of a car is affected by its shape – air resistance is kept to a minimum by making the car low and with a smooth, curving shape. The wings, or spoilers, seen on Grand Prix cars and some sports cars produce a downforce which improves road holding at high speeds.

The safety frame of a Formula One car is strengthened to protect the driver during a crash. Grand Prix safety improvements mean crashes are now rarely fatal.

The 1930s saw the development of the super-charger, a device which meant that small capacity engines could be literally 'blown' into much more powerful machines. It does this by increasing the amount of air taken into the engine to boost performance. This led to a split in the classification of racing cars, and after the Second World War unsupercharged engines could be as big as 4.5 litres, whereas supercharged cars had to be 1.5 litres or less.

But it was in 1977 that the biggest impact on motor racing was first felt – the turbocharged Renault. Like superchargers, turbo power vastly increased the power output of an engine, only much more markedly. In turbocharged engines, a pump driven by the engine's exhaust increases the pressure on the gases inside the engine. The high pressure increases the force of the combustion inside the engine's cylinders. Turbocharged cars can go considerably faster than cars with the same size, non-turbocharged engines.

Safety standards in today's motor racing events are stringent, but there are still accidents and the history of Grand Prix racing has seen many fatalities. The driver's cockpit is now strengthened by carbon fibre able to withstand horrific-looking crashes – on impact, major parts break away from the racing car in such a way that drivers are not injured by flying debris. Every car has a sophisticated high-pressure fire extinguishing system, which can put out fires that often follow a crash.

Gravelled areas on fast corners, which are designed to slow down cars, and wide run-off areas are standard features of racing tracks around the world. On modern circuits marshalling is more effective and circuit organization much more co-ordinated, with officials, doctors and accident and first-aid equipment situated all round the track.

Powerboat racing is now becoming more popular, both offshore and on circuits, where old docks and waterways are used. Some of today's powerboats are capable of speeds in excess of 220 kph and the acceleration from their 2-litre engines is a phenomenal 0-160 kph in just 4.2 seconds. Any powerboat, including a ski boat with a top speed of 65 kph can, given

Millions are spent on perfecting motor bikes for the racing circuit.

choppy conditions, become airborne. However, in races, time spent in the air is time spent without the push of the engines, so it is avoided as much as possible.

Technology has done much to increase the speed and power of the motor bike, too. The first motor-cycle races were recorded at the end of the nineteenth century, but because of a speed limit of 32 kph in Britain, they were forced to look for 'off-road' circuits and 'offshore' races, such as the Isle of Man, where the famed TT (Tourist Trophy) Races have been staged since 1907.

The first motor bikes were crude, single-cylinder machines, with 5 cm diameter tyres, mudguards and pedals to help the riders up steep hills. In 1920, a four-stroke Sunbeam motor bike completed the 364.5 km race at an average speed of 83.38 kph. In 1984, a 750 cc Honda completed the course at an average speed of 190.35 kph. The motor bike was built to high-tech racing specifications including a two-part radiator system for maximum cooling power, electronic fuel injection, and a lightweight metal alloy frame.

### Racing boat designs

Racing boats have two basic hull designs – displacement and planing. Motorboats with displacement hulls ride in the water. Those with planing hulls skim over the water's surface. Hydroplanes are the most common planing boats. The bottom of the hull is flat or slightly curved. A flat-bottom boat has gently sloped sides. The boat may have engines either inside or outside the hull. A tunnel hull has long 'floats' that extend the length of each side, creating a 'tunnel' down the middle. A V-bottom hull has steeply slanted sides with a pointed bottom. These hulls perform well in rough water.

Hydroplane

V-bottom hull

Flatbottom hull

Tunnel hull

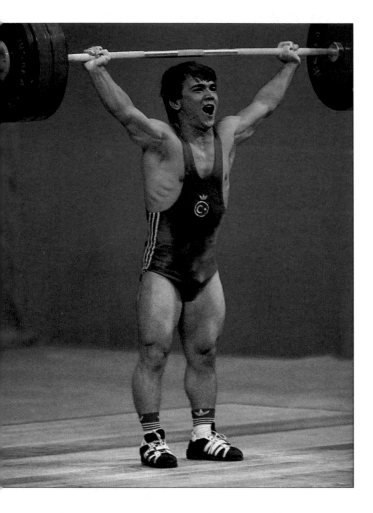

Positive drug tests marred the 1988 Olympic weightlifting competition.

Technology has not been a completely beneficial force on the world of sport. As sport has become more competitive, prize money and prestige have grown, and thus the incentive to win has vastly increased. Technology has played a key role in developing short cuts to success, in simple terms, cheating.

The use of performance-enhancing drugs has spread since the late 1960s, when the 'power' athletes, notably bodybuilders, weightlifters, field event throwers and American footballers, began experimenting with them. Sportsmen and sportswomen turn to drugs in the belief that they will help them to run faster or longer, and help them to train better or build up muscles.

Drug taking has had a chilling knock-on effect in world sport, as athletes began to think that if they did not take something they would never win. As one notable drug taker admitted: 'If you're not on anything it's like lining up on the blocks wearing trainers when everyone else is in spikes.'

• **Stimulants** are aimed at giving athletes a short high, leaving them in an ultra wakeful state.

• **Steroids** and hormones help build up body muscle and encourage the development of body tissue.

• **Narcotic analgesics** are strong painkillers.

• **Betablockers** slow down the heart rate and encourage calmness.

• **Diuretics** reduce weight by removing water from the body.

Many performance-enhancing drugs are banned by the sporting bodies such as the International Olympic Committee (IOC) and the International Amateur Athletics Federation (IAAF) – the IAAF's current banned list extends to hundreds of drugs in many different categories. The positive testing of Canadian sprinter Ben Johnson was something of a windfall for the authorities – it came at a time when they were starting to address the drugs problem. Not only was Johnson the greatest sprinter of all time and the reigning world champion, but he was caught in the full glare of the world's media after smashing the world record and winning the 100 m sprint at the 1988 Seoul Olympics.

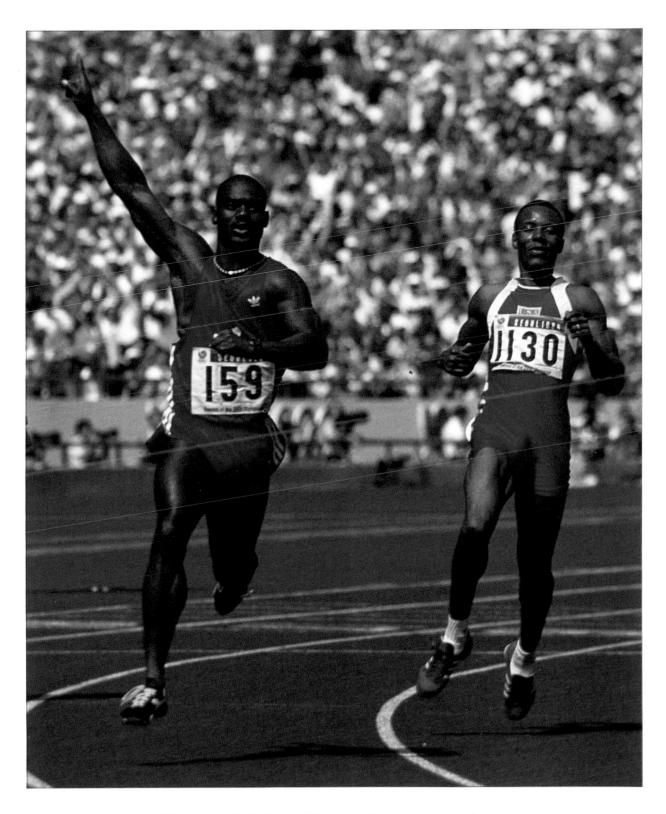

Ben Johnson wins the 100 m at the 1988 Seoul Olympics. He was then tested positive for the banned steroid, Stanozolol, and stripped of his gold medal.

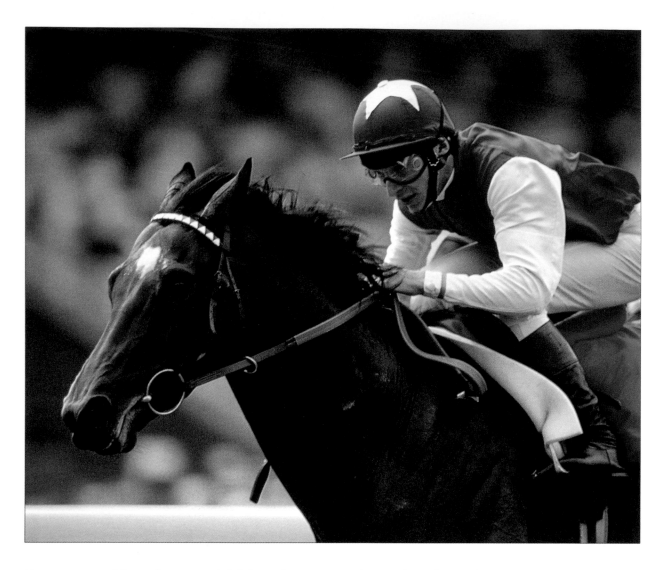

Humans are not the only racers at risk from drugs — race horses have been given drugs to improve their performances as well.

Johnson had been taking steroids for some years. He said they enabled him to train longer and harder, build up muscle and come into competitions far more aggressively. In terms of carrying the anti-drug message, the Johnson episode did much to focus attention on improving drug detection and rooting out the cheats.

Johnson served his punishment (a two-year ban) and returned to athletic competition. He planned to race at the Olympic Games in Barcelona in 1992. Some people think all drug takers should be banned from competitive athletics for life, while others believe that they should be given a second chance once they have proved they are no longer taking performance-enhancing drugs.

The side effects of taking steroids, the most widely used drug in sport, can be very serious and in some cases have caused deaths. A twenty-six-year-old bodybuilder died recently from liver cancer after taking steroids for some years. They can also contribute to the risk of heart disorders.

Stimulant overdoses have also caused sports deaths in recent decades: a Danish cyclist died during an Olympic race in 1960, and a world championship cyclist died during the Tour de France in 1967. In both cases the drug responsible was amphetamine, which is used to intensify performance, and helps athletes to shrug off sports injuries.

Blood doping is another method that is used to improve performance. An athlete has red blood cells removed from his or her blood, and when the body has replaced the cells itself, the removed cells are returned to the blood. With an increase in red blood cells, the athlete has an increased but temporary advantage because he or she is able to carry more oxygen in the blood, which aids performance in long distance events.

Drug detection was first introduced at the Olympics, in Mexico, in 1968, although the first steroid tests were not conducted until 1976.

Urine samples are collected randomly – in training or competition – tested for banned substances and a disciplinary procedure put into action if even the smallest trace is found.

In 1986, IOC-accredited laboratories around the world discovered 687 banned substances in the course of their work. The following year, the figure had risen to 924, while in 1988 it totalled 1,353 (which included the Olympics), and in 1989 (a quieter year for athletics) the figure was 1,341.

Despite the Johnson saga and the vast sums of money that have been spent on drug detection techniques, it seems that drug taking is still as big a menace as ever, and sports authorities around the world are now discussing what new means are available to stop what has become an extremely undesirable development.

A laboratory technician checks samples in test tubes. There are many drug-testing laboratories operating around the world.

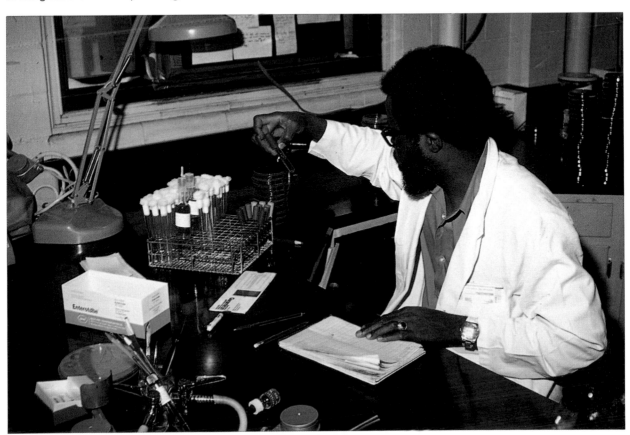

Television has contributed greatly to the development and popularization of sport. Before global television coverage was possible, sporting events were staged before a 'live' crowd and relayed to millions of others in the early days by newspapers alone, and then from the 1920s by radio. Today, every major international sporting event – and thousands of smaller ones – are beamed into our homes via satellite.

In 1936, when the BBC began its first regular television service from London, *The Times* newspaper suggested that television would 'give the opportunity to satisfy an eager public' and that 'all the doings of the great world would take on new life and interest'. The newspaper was right, and in the first years of television broadcasting, the management of the BBC looked upon sport as a good way of guaranteeing a mass audience. But it took time

Television cameras ready to capture the best soccer action. Instant slow-motion replay is a feature of sports coverage.

The television coverage has improved thanks to the use of remote-controlled cameras which are positioned to give an unusual view of a sports event.

for television technology to come to terms with sports coverage, first in recorded form, and then live transmissions of major events.

In 1939, America's NBC television station transmitted its first outside broadcast – a baseball game between Princeton and Columbia Universities. In those days, the pictures were not very clear or sharp, and the best sports coverage was restricted to small arena events, such as boxing and tennis, rather than large pitch sports, such as soccer and baseball. It was not until the 1948 Olympics that the BBC managed to improve its cameras enough to make coverage of field sports worthwhile. The Image Orthicon camera had three interchangeable lenses and a viewfinder which, unlike previous cameras, gave the image the right way up. This made it easier for the cameramen to get the best pictures, and the standard of coverage improved.

In the 1950s and 1960s, soccer matches were covered by just four large cameras and with no action or slow-motion replays. These came at the end of the 1960s, and could only be used after an event had been recorded and then edited down to produce a report which showed the highlights. Today, there is instant slow-motion replay for any part of a live game, and ITV's *The Match* soccer coverage uses twelve cameras to give television viewers a much better view of the game.

The medium on which sport is recorded has also changed. Sixteen millimetre film was replaced by 2 inch (51.8 mm) magnetic tape, which was physically cut during the editing process. Today, half-inch tape (12.7 mm) is the norm, which can be edited at the touch of a button. Digital tape, which records pictures as computerized digits, will greatly improve the quality and clarity of pictures.

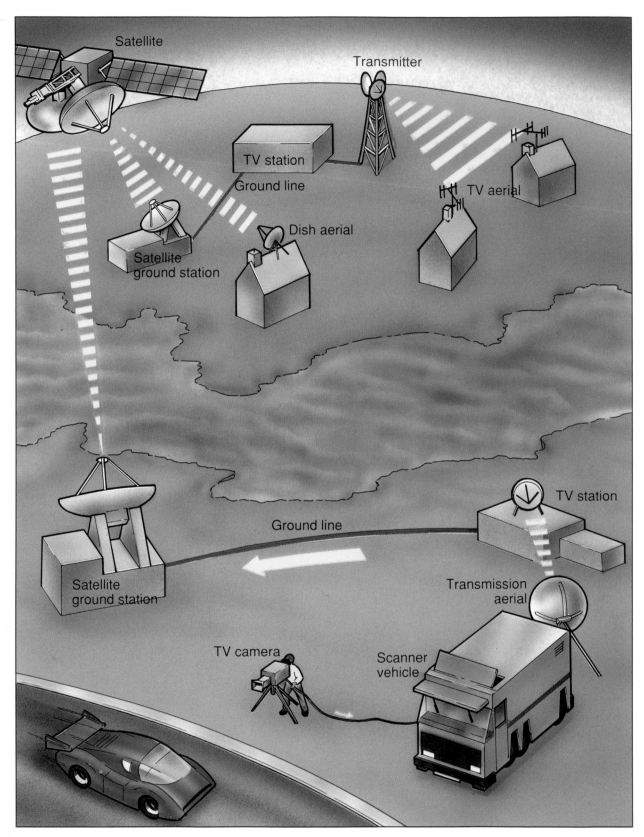

Satellite

Transmitter

TV station

Ground line

Satellite
ground station

Dish aerial

TV aerial

Satellite
ground station

Ground line

TV station

Transmission
aerial

TV camera

Scanner
vehicle

A major landmark in television coverage is the use of satellite technology to relay pictures around the world. Satellites were first used to send pictures from the Tokyo Olympics, in 1964. But the receiving country had little or no control over which events were received. Since then, satellite technology has improved beyond recognition and the number of satellites has increased greatly, so that any sports event in any country can be transmitted to our television screens. At the 1988 Seoul Olympics in Korea, most major broadcasters secured in advance the use of satellites and used them to send pictures of the events that would be of interest to their viewers in their own countries.

The first colour transmissions started in America in 1953. In Britain, the BBC introduced colour pictures in 1967, while in Australia colour television was introduced in the early 1970s and coincided with the opening of the Sydney Opera House. However, colour television did not catch on immediately in Britain. It was not until the mid-1970s that most households had a colour television set. By then sport had taken on a new meaning. Soccer, rugby, winter sports, the Olympics and, of course, snooker, looked so much more realistic.

Satellite television has brought a new dimension to sports enthusiasts around the world, as there are channels which specialize in transmitting major sports events. Sky Television, now British Sky Broadcasting, has used mini cameras and advanced sound equipment to move sports coverage forward. For example, in cricket, it has used microphones around the wicket and mini cameras planted in the stumps to give a new dimension to coverage.

Mini cameras are a relatively new idea, but over the last few years they have been gradually introduced into many different sports. They are about the size of a cigar and can be mounted with clamps almost anywhere – goalmouths, Formula One racing cars, ice hockey pucks and skateboards, for example.

New advances in television technology will add significantly to the enjoyment of sports fans. The wide screen and high definition television with its cinemascope picture, could mean the end of the ordinary sets and the introduction of screens, like mini cinemas, in the home. Added to that will be stereo sound, with special sound effects. The development of television sports coverage has always been to try and bring the event to the viewer – soon the viewer will feel as if he or she is actually at the event.

**Opposite** The satellite has revolutionized the television industry – now events can be seen live from anywhere in the world.

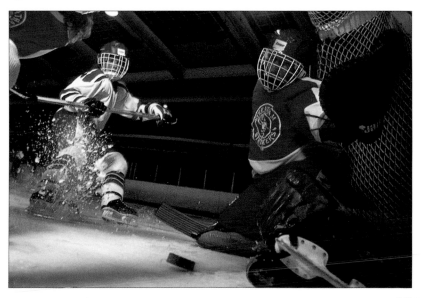

**Right** A mini camera in an ice hockey goal shoots some close-up match action.

# Glossary

**Amphetamine** One of several drugs that increase physical and mental activity, prevent sleep and decrease appetite. In athletics, the drug increases alertness and may quicken reflex action.

**Barnum's Circus** A circus founded by the most famous showman of his time, P. T. Barnum. The circus opened in 1871 and Barnum later called it 'The Greatest Show on Earth'.

**Bobsleigh** A racing sledge for two or more people, with a steering mechanism enabling the driver to direct it down a steep, icy course.

**Carbon fibre** Fine, black silky threads, each thinner than a human hair, that when used as a reinforcement can make a material much tougher.

**Cinder track** An old-style running track made from the material that is left after the burning of coal or coke. Today's running tracks are made from artificial materials.

**Coach** A trainer or instructor who prepares sportsmen and sportswomen for competition.

**Concourse** A large open space in a stadium where people can gather before taking their seats.

**Digital** Concerned with numbers or digits. Digital tape is a magnetic tape on which pictures and sounds can be recorded digitally, giving high-quality reproduction.

**Executive box** An exclusive room or compartment in a stadium which overlooks the playing area. Business people often entertain their clients in these boxes.

**Four-stroke engine** An internal combustion engine in which a piston makes four strokes for every explosion. In a four-stroke cycle, a piston moves down, sucking fuel into the cylinder (1). The piston rises again, compressing the mixture (2). A spark ignites it and the gases produced force the piston down (3). Finally, the piston rises pushing the burnt gases out of the cylinder (4).

**Fuel injection** A system for introducing fuel directly into the combustion chambers of an internal combustion engine.

**Gladiatorial combat** A fight between trained warriors to entertain the ancient Romans. Most gladiators were prisoners of war, slaves or criminals. Often they were forced to fight to death in these contests.

**Grand Prix** This is a French term which means 'big prize', and is any of a series of races in which Formula One cars compete.

**Graphite** A soft, black material which, in carbon fibre form, is used for tough, lightweight sports equipment.

**Injection moulding** A method of shaping an object by introducing a fluid under pressure into a mould.

**Lycra** A type of synthetic elastic fabric and fibre which is used for running suits and swimming costumes.

**Magnetic tape** A long strip of plastic tape which has been impregnated or coated with crystals of iron oxide. The tape is used to record sound or video signals.

**Minerals** A class of inorganic substances, many of which are needed by the body in very small amounts, such as iodine, copper, manganese, iron and cobalt.

**Nutritionist** A person who has studied the role of food in relation to the processes that depend on its absorption by the body – growth, energy production and repair of body tissues, for example.

**Psychologist** A person who is engaged in the study of the mind and human behaviour.

**Satellite** A man-made device orbiting around the earth – a communications satellite is used for receiving, amplifying and re-transmitting radio or television signals.

**Starting block** An adjustable device with pads against which a sprinter braces his or her feet in a crouch start.

**Steroid** One of a large group of compounds that is used by athletes to build up muscles and encourage the development of body tissue.

**Synthetic** Artificially created substances in which two or more elements are combined to make a compound. Plastics and fibres such as acrylic and nylon are synthetic materials.

**Tournament** A sporting competition in which contestants play a series of games to determine an overall winner.

**Venue** The place where a sports event is held.

**Vitamin** One of a group of chemical compounds that the human body needs in small amounts.

# Further reading

Baker, W J *Sport in the Western World* (Rowman & Little, 1983)

Duncanson, N *The Fastest Men on Earth* (Collins, 1988)

*Guinness Book of American Football* (Guinness, 1989)

*Guinness Book of Cricket* (Guinness, 1983)

*Guinness Book of Motor Racing* (Guinness, 1989)

Graham, I *Racing Cars* (Franklin Watts, 1989)

Kerrod, R *Motorcycles* (Franklin Watts, 1989)

Lambert, M *TV and Video Technology* (Wayland, 1989)

Mohan, J *Drugs, Steroids and Sport* (Franklin Watts, 1988)

# Acknowledgements

The author would like to thank the following for their help in the writing of this book: Adidas (UK) Ltd, Amateur Rowing Association, Amateur Swimming Association, British Association for the Advancement of Science, Cantabrian, Dunlop-Slazenger, IAAF, Lonsdale, Motorsport Magazine, National Football League, Omega Electronics Ltd, Ontario House, Alan Pascoe Associates, Raleigh, Reebok, Speedo, Sports Council, Wimbledon Tennis Museum.

The publishers would like to thank the following for allowing their photographs to be reproduced in this book: Aldus Archive 25 (bottom); Bob Allen 12; Allsport 4 (bottom, Simon Bruty), 5 (Adrien Murrell), 6 (bottom, Mike Powell), 9 (Bob Martin), 10 (top, Didier Givois), 14, 15 (top, Mike Powell), 16 (Mike Powell), 17 (Kurt Amsler), 19 (Jean-Pierre Lenfant), 22 (left, Howard Boylan), 26 (Jean-Marc Barey), 28 (Mike Powell), 29 (Gray Mortimore), 30 (David Cannon), 34 (Pascal Rondeau), 37 (Mike Powell), 38 (Jun Nicholson), 41 (Ruussell Cheyne), 43 (Bob Martin); W L Gore & Associates 15 (bottom); Omega 23; Science Photo Library 39; Sporting Pictures 4; Topham 14 (left), 36; Ultra Sport (UK) Ltd 18, 20, 21; Wembley Stadium Ltd 6 (top); ZEFA *cover*, 11, 25 (top), 27, 31. Artwork by Brian Davey

# Index